Step 1
Go to www.openlightbox.com

Step 2
Enter this unique code
APFSYGLFE

Step 3
Explore your interactive eBook!

Your interactive eBook comes with...

Audio
Listen to the entire book read aloud

Videos
Watch informative video clips

Weblinks
Gain additional information for research

Try This!
Complete activities and hands-on experiments

Key Words
Study vocabulary, and complete a matching word activity

Quizzes
Test your knowledge

Slideshows
View images and captions

Share
Share titles within your Learning Management System (LMS) or Library Circulation System

Citation
Create bibliographical references following APA, CMOS, and MLA styles

AV2 is optimized for use on any device

This title is part of our AV2 digital subscription

1-Year K–2 Subscription
ISBN 978-1-7911-3310-8

Access hundreds of AV2 titles with our digital subscription.
Sign up for a FREE trial at **www.openlightbox.com/trial**

The digital components of this book are guaranteed to stay active for at least five years from the date of publication.

Dachshund

CONTENTS

  2 Interactive eBook Code
  4 Bold and Curious
  6 Small Dogs
  8 Coat Colors
 10 Growing Up
 12 Hunting Dogs
 14 Exercise
 16 Grooming
 18 Food and Attention
 20 Staying Healthy
 22 Incredible Dachshunds
 24 Sight Words

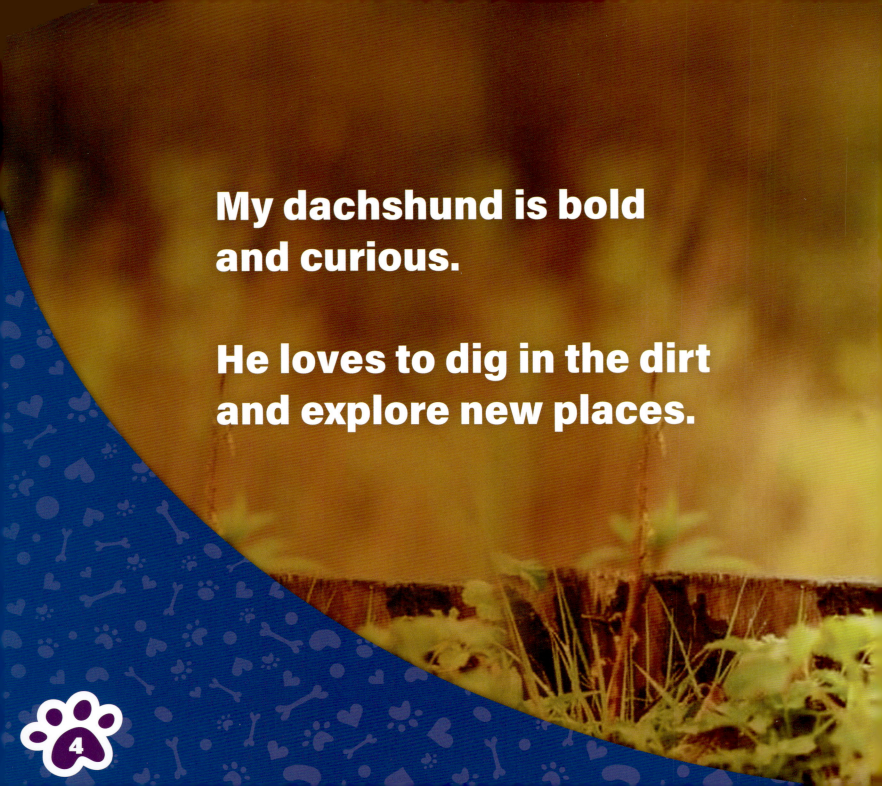

My dachshund is bold and curious.

He loves to dig in the dirt and explore new places.

Dachshunds are small dogs. They have short legs and long, narrow bodies.

Dog Shoulder Heights

Chihuahua
Up to 8 inches
(20 centimeters)

Dachshund
Up to 9 inches
(23 cm)

Pembroke Welsh Corgi
Up to 12 inches
(30 cm)

Dachshunds can have short fur, long fur, or stiff, wiry hair.

My dachshund has a short black and tan coat. Others may have red or cream coats.

Dachshund puppies are small with soft, fluffy coats.

Their coats may change color as they grow.

Where in the World

Dachshunds come from Germany. The name *dachshund* means "badger dog" in German.

Dachshunds were bred to hunt small animals, such as badgers and rabbits.

Their long bodies helped them fit into underground burrows.

My dachshund likes to go on adventures.

He enjoys sniffing around.

I brush my dachshund's smooth coat to keep his fur healthy.

Dachshunds with long or wiry hair need to be groomed often.

I feed my dachshund twice a day.

I also give him plenty of attention. He likes to play hide and seek.

I take my dachshund to the veterinarian at least once a year.

The veterinarian helps keep my dog healthy.

Dog Breed Popularity in the United States

#5
Poodle

#6
Dachshund

#7
English Bulldog

20

Standard dachshunds weigh about **16** to **32 pounds** (7 to 15 kilograms). Miniature dachshunds weigh **11 pounds** (5 kg) or **less**.

Dachshunds come in two sizes. These are **standard** and **miniature**.

SIGHT WORDS

Research has shown that as much as 65 percent of all written material published in English is made up of 300 words. These 300 words cannot be taught using pictures or learned by sounding them out. They must be recognized by sight. This book contains 61 common sight words to help young readers improve their reading fluency and comprehension. This book also teaches young readers several important content words, such as proper nouns. These words are paired with pictures to aid in learning and improve understanding.

Page	Sight Words First Appearance
4	and, he, in, is, my, new, places, the, to
6	are, have, long, small, they, up
9	a, can, has, may, or, others
10	with
11	as, change, come, from, grow, means, name, their, where, world
12	animals, into, such, them, were
14	around, go, likes, on
15	day, every, him, I, keep, take, walks
17	be, his, need, often
19	also, give, of, play
20	at, helps, once, states, year

Page	Content Words First Appearance
4	dachshund, dirt
6	bodies, Chihuahua, dogs heights, legs, Pembroke Welsh corgi, shoulder
9	coat, fur, hair
10	puppies
11	badger, color, German, Germany
12	burrows, rabbits
14	adventures
19	attention, hide and seek
20	breed, English bulldog, poodle, popularity, United States, veterinarian

Published by Lightbox Learning Inc.
276 5th Avenue, Suite 704 #917
New York, NY 10001
Website: www.openlightbox.com

Copyright ©2026 Lightbox Learning Inc.
All rights reserved. No part of this publication may be reproduced, stored in a retrieval system, or transmitted in any form or by any means, electronic, mechanical, photocopying, recording, or otherwise, without the prior written permission of the publisher.

Library of Congress Control Number: 2024057205

ISBN 979-8-8745-2153-0 (hardcover)
ISBN 979-8-8745-2155-4 (softcover)
ISBN 979-8-8745-2154-7 (static multi-user eBook)
ISBN 979-8-8745-2157-8 (interactive multi-user eBook)

012025
100924

Printed in Guangzhou, China
1 2 3 4 5 6 7 8 9 0   29 28 27 26 25

Project Coordinator: Priyanka Das
Designer: Jean Faye Rodriguez

Every reasonable effort has been made to trace ownership and to obtain permission to reprint copyright material. The publisher would be pleased to have any errors or omissions brought to its attention so that they may be corrected in subsequent printings.

The publisher acknowledges Getty Images and Shutterstock as its primary image suppliers for this title.